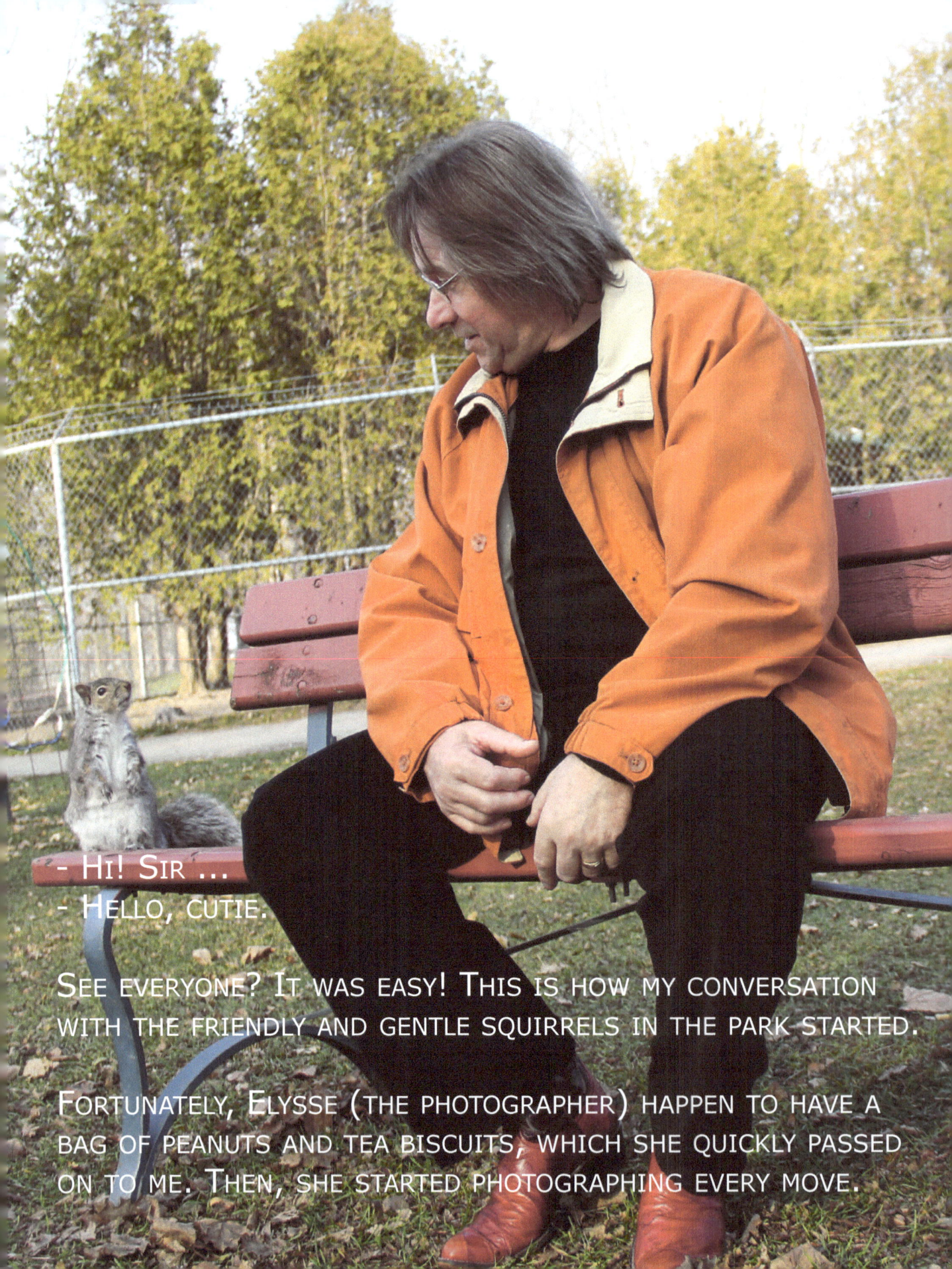

- HI! SIR ...
- HELLO, CUTIE.

SEE EVERYONE? IT WAS EASY! THIS IS HOW MY CONVERSATION WITH THE FRIENDLY AND GENTLE SQUIRRELS IN THE PARK STARTED.

FORTUNATELY, ELYSSE (THE PHOTOGRAPHER) HAPPEN TO HAVE A BAG OF PEANUTS AND TEA BISCUITS, WHICH SHE QUICKLY PASSED ON TO ME. THEN, SHE STARTED PHOTOGRAPHING EVERY MOVE.

PHOTOGRAPHED STORY

The Squirrels and I

An afternoon in the Park

KLAUS D. EMRICH

PHOTOGRAPHY ELYSSE POETIS

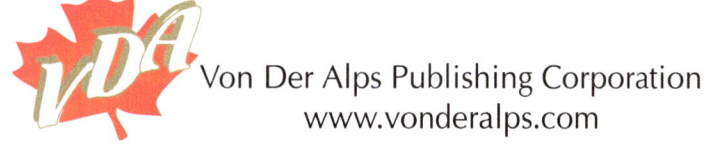

Von Der Alps Publishing Corporation
www.vonderalps.com

The Squirrels and I

Author - Klaus D. Emrich

Photographer - Elysse Poetis

Copyright and Intellectual/Creative Property of the
author/model Klaus D. Emrich and photographer Elysse Poetis
starting with © 2014 and beyond.

First original published in September 2014 by
Von Der Alps Publishing Corporation, CANADA.

www.vonderalps.com

Canadian Cataloguing in Publication Data
ISBN 978-0-9936867-1-9

Printed in USA

Dedication

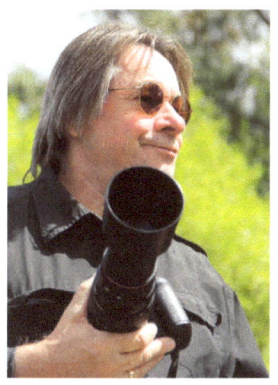 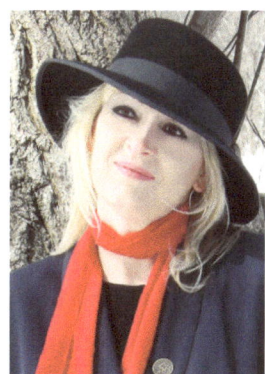

dedicate this book to Elysse, who in the last decade with kindness and persistence inspired me to once again, like in my childhood, embrace nature and its infinite beauty.

Modern science is mimicking nature in order to improve our lifes. Stronger and smarter materials are being discovered and manipulated every day at the smallest scale. The infinite map of nanoscale architecture is our cozy Mother Nature. Finally, we came to the clear conclusion that nature is the teacher - Its fields are the class rooms - We are its students. And Elysse could see it since she was a child herself, attracted to photography, poetry and story writing. She is my wife and my best friend with whom I love exploring the natural world, read about it, write about it, and photograph it.

The Award Winning energetic and infectiously curious Elysse is the author of multiple books on Amazon. She writes true stories, fiction, poetry and fantasy. Some of her books are strictly photography. Every day she reminds me how much she appreciates having me as her husband and best friend, to take her hand and go for long walks in the nature as much as possible. We enjoy every season, day and night. Overall, we wish humanity a brilliant, healthy future.

Klaus D. Emrich

About the squirrels

These poofy tail beauties belong to a family called "Sciuridae." Some of the members of this large and colourful family are:
- Chipmunks
- Tree Squirrels
- Ground Squirrels
- Flying Squirrels
- Prairie Dogs
- Marmots
- Woodchucks, etc.

The North American Grey Squirrel in Ontario, CANADA

NOTE: The subfamilies of the above members could incorporate numerous species each. (Takes time and curiosity in order to discover their history. There is a lot of fun involved).

Considering that squirrels are very sensitive, playful, highly intelligent, gentle and super-friendly, trust and friendship between them and humans can develop over a short period of time in a peaceful environment. They like soft voices. As city residents, squirrels enjoy food like: roasted peanuts, buds, maple keys, berries, fruit, insects, etc. Their nests are fancy, build in the shape of a basket made out of leafs and twigs, safe from predators on the ground, up in the treetops. If safe and well feed squirrels can live as long as cats and dogs.

Our neighbourhoods are super-sources of fun and information available for us all to observe and explore.

The Squirrels and I

On a beautiful Fall day, my wife Elysse and I decided to go out for a walk in the park and take some pictures. She also suggested to take roasted peanuts and seeds with us, just in case the little wild animals where hungry. In Ontario, CANADA, we have a large variety of squirrels, every colour, big and small.

As soon as we arrived in the park the squirrels surrounded us in the hope to get some food, and we where trilled with all the attention. And so, the show started! Elysse took picture after picture, while I had the pleasure to interact with the little creatures and feed them.

Due to the wonderful experience, I will forever recommend to you all: children, teenagers, young adults, parents and grandparents, to get out in your community parks and observe the nature with all its glory. There is nothing more rewarding than the discovery that these little squirrels are no different than our domestic cats and dogs.

Highly intelligent and super-gentle, the squirrels have the ability to charm and trust. They immediately wash their faces and tails in order to show their beauty and get that special peanut.

The photographs in this fun-book demonstrate that harmony between humans and tiny wild life is enjoyable.

Klaus D. Emrich

The Squirrels and I

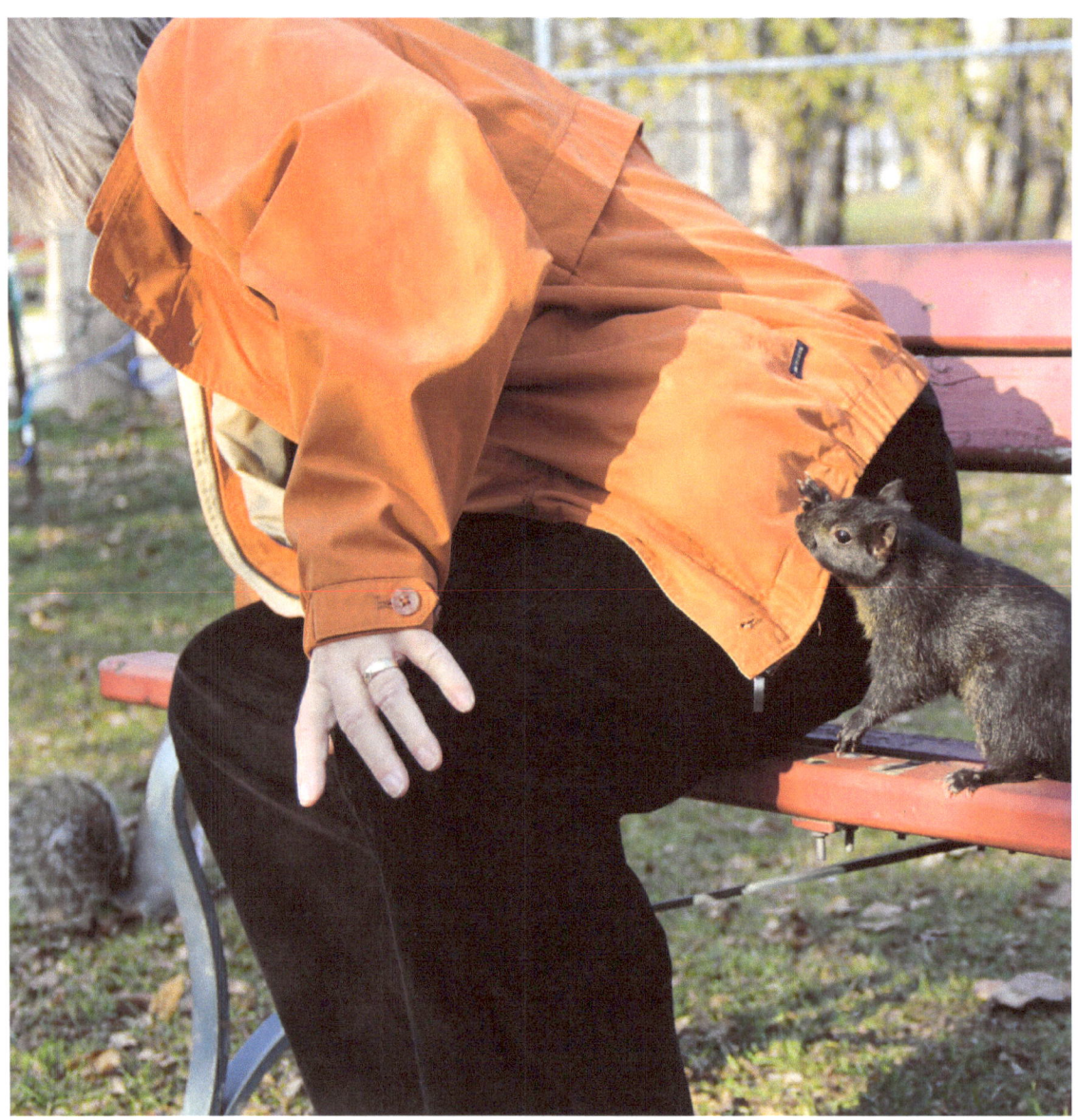

It is feeding time for the squirrels.

The Squirrels and I

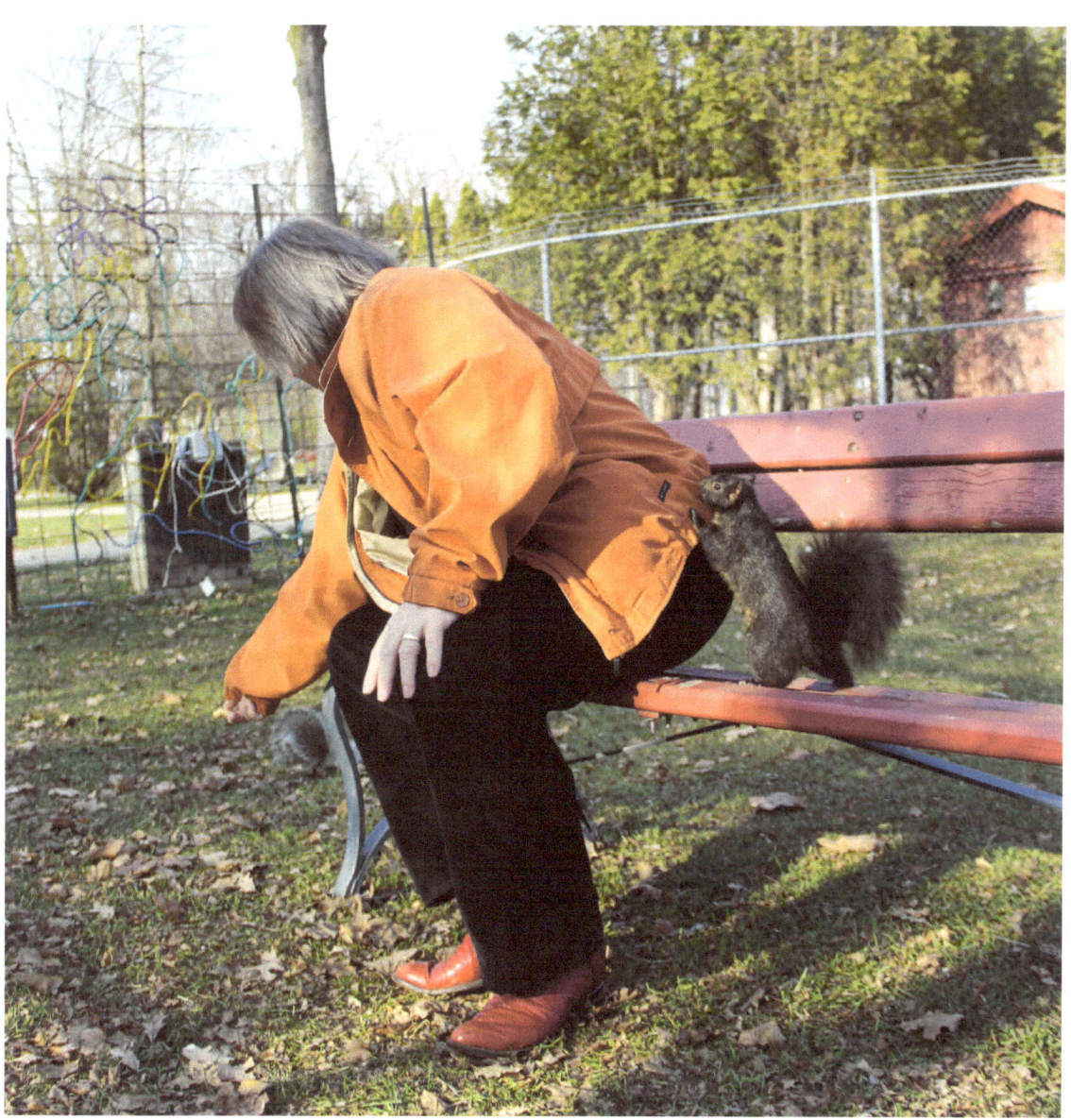

Sir, I'm behind you! Please, do not forget me.

The Squirrels and I

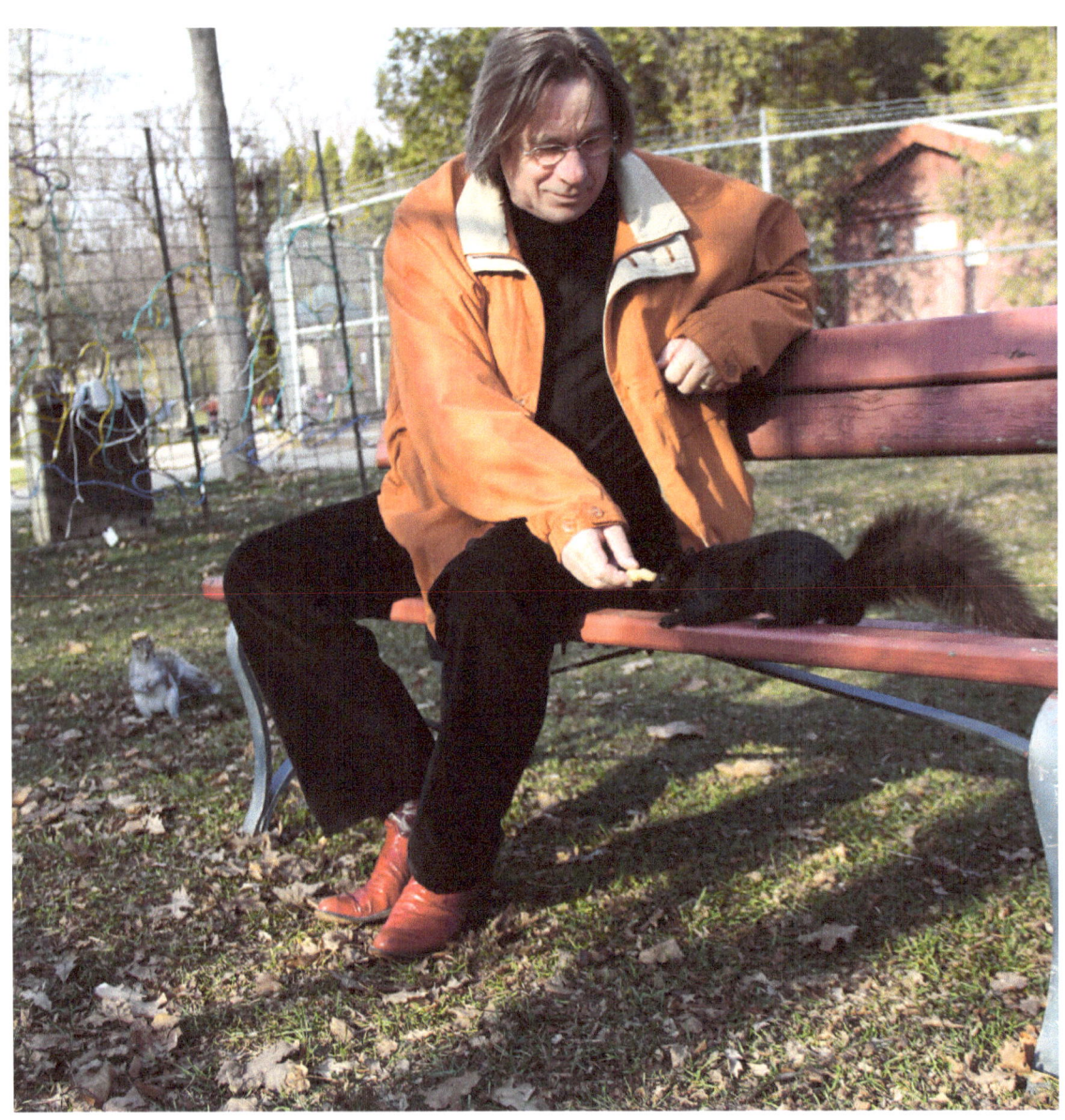

You see? I did not forget you, my tiny friend.

The Squirrels and I

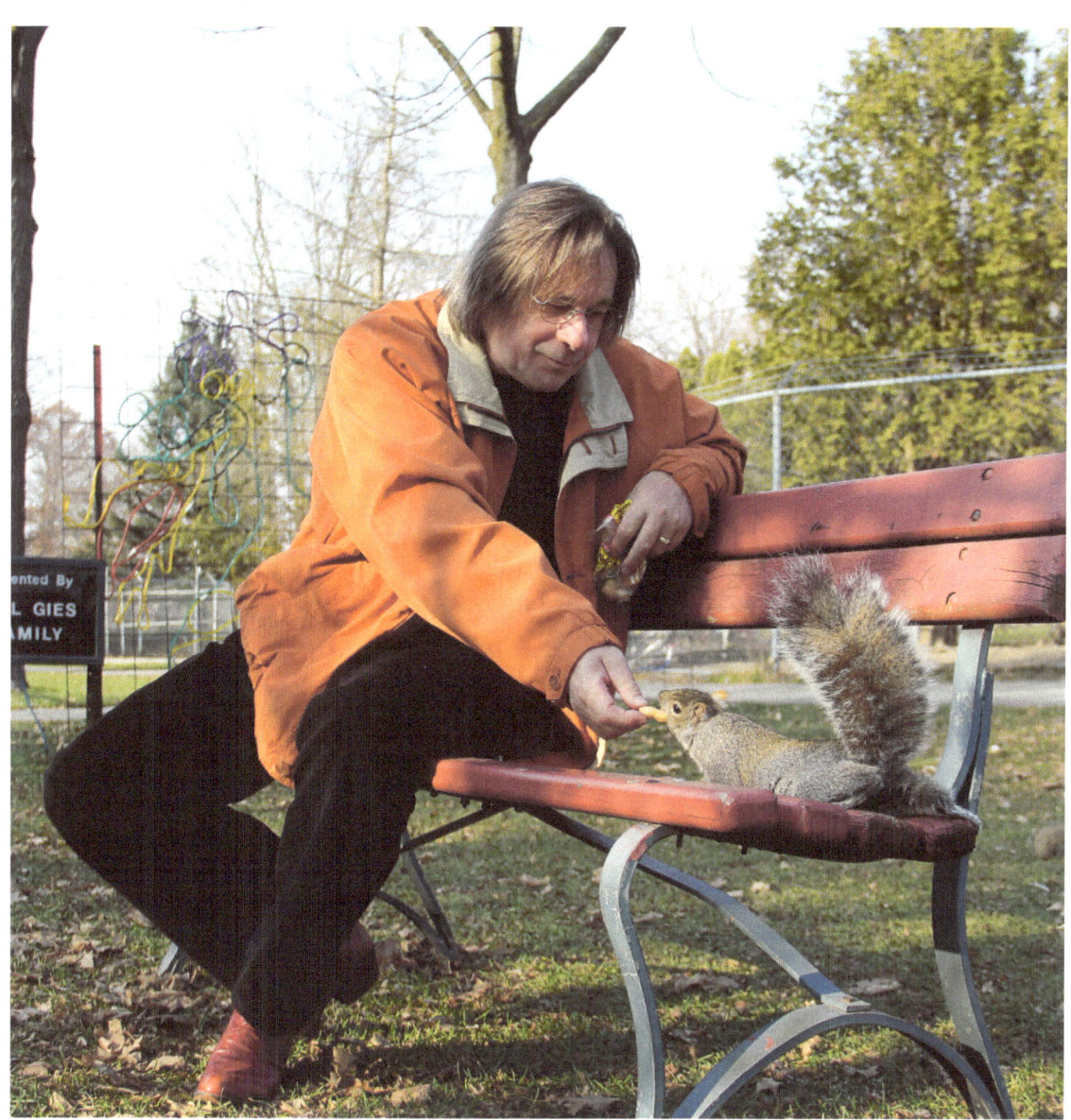

You little charmer ... You too will get your well deserved peanut.

The Squirrels and I

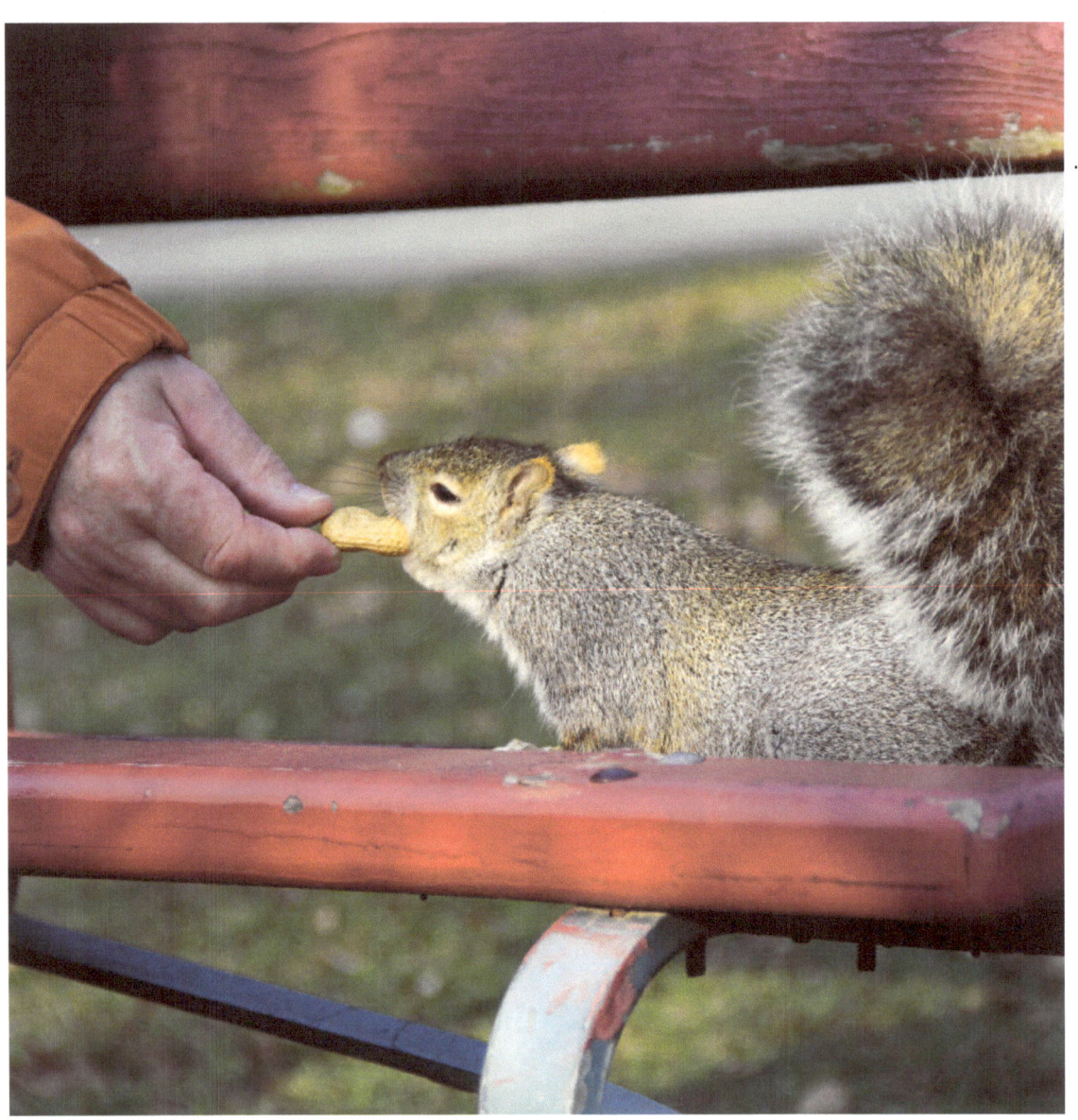

Oh, it smells so good ...

The Squirrels and I

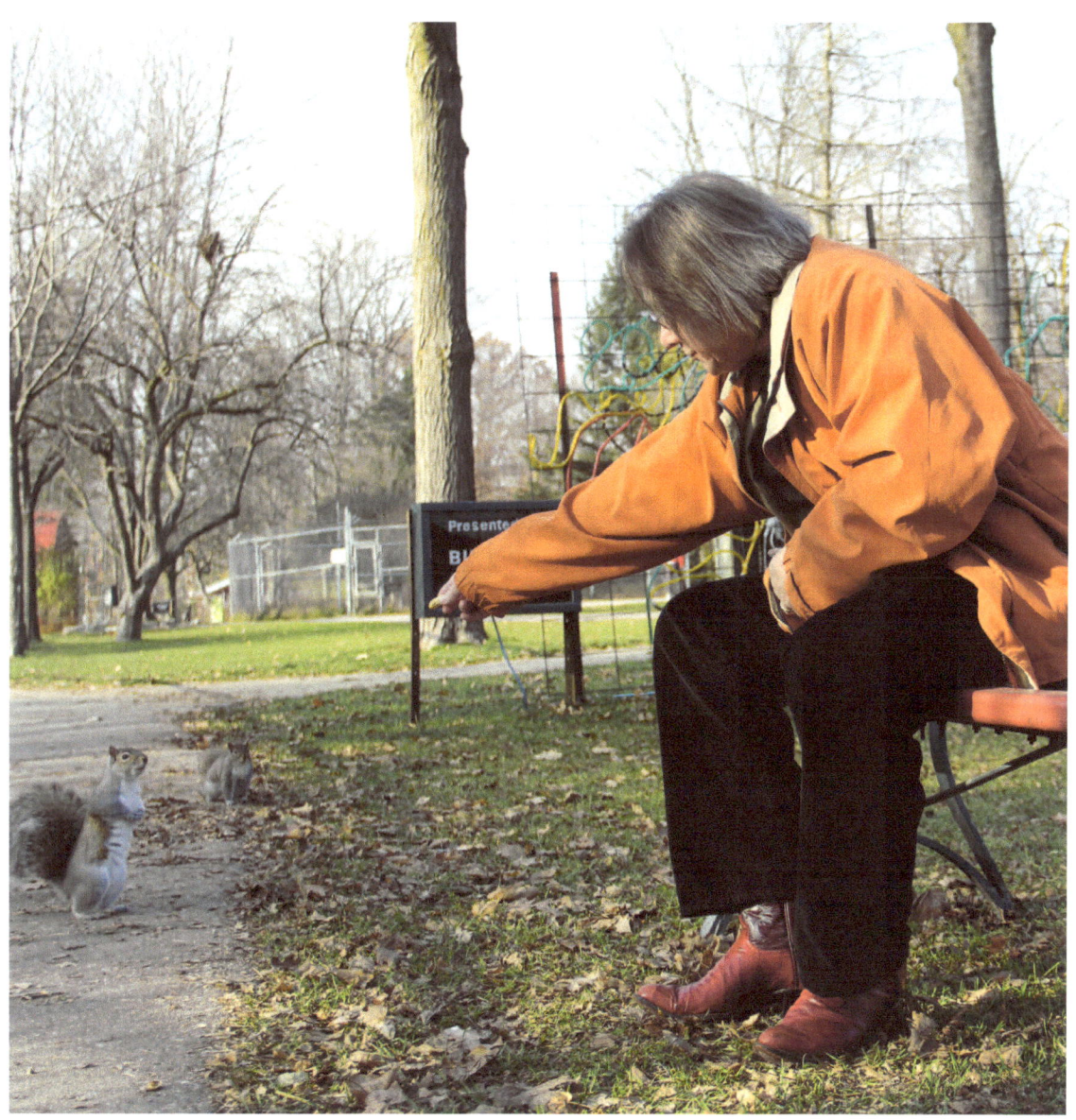

Hi guys! Don't be shy. Here are your peanuts.

The Squirrels and I

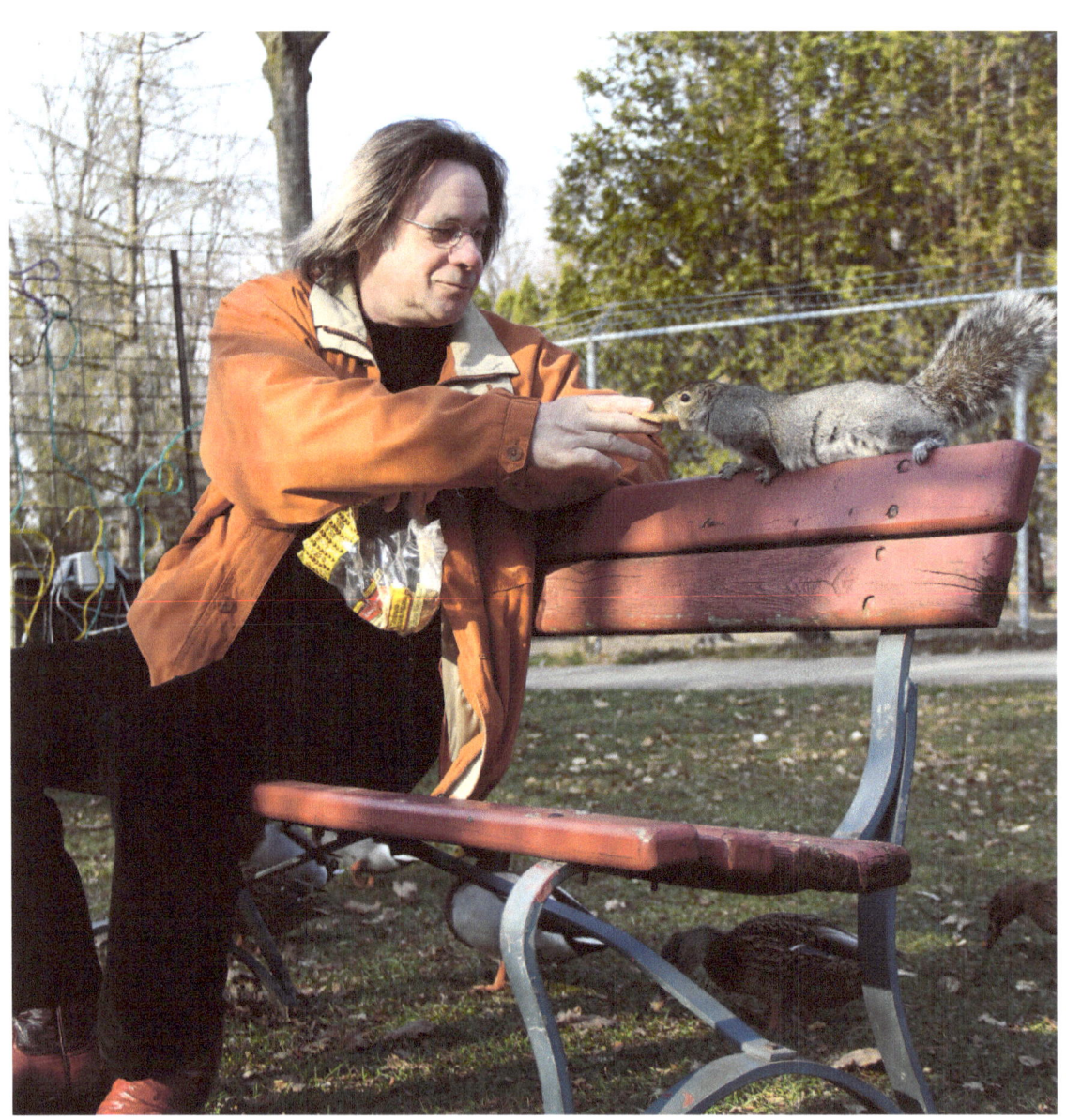

Now for dessert, tea biscuits!

The Squirrels and I

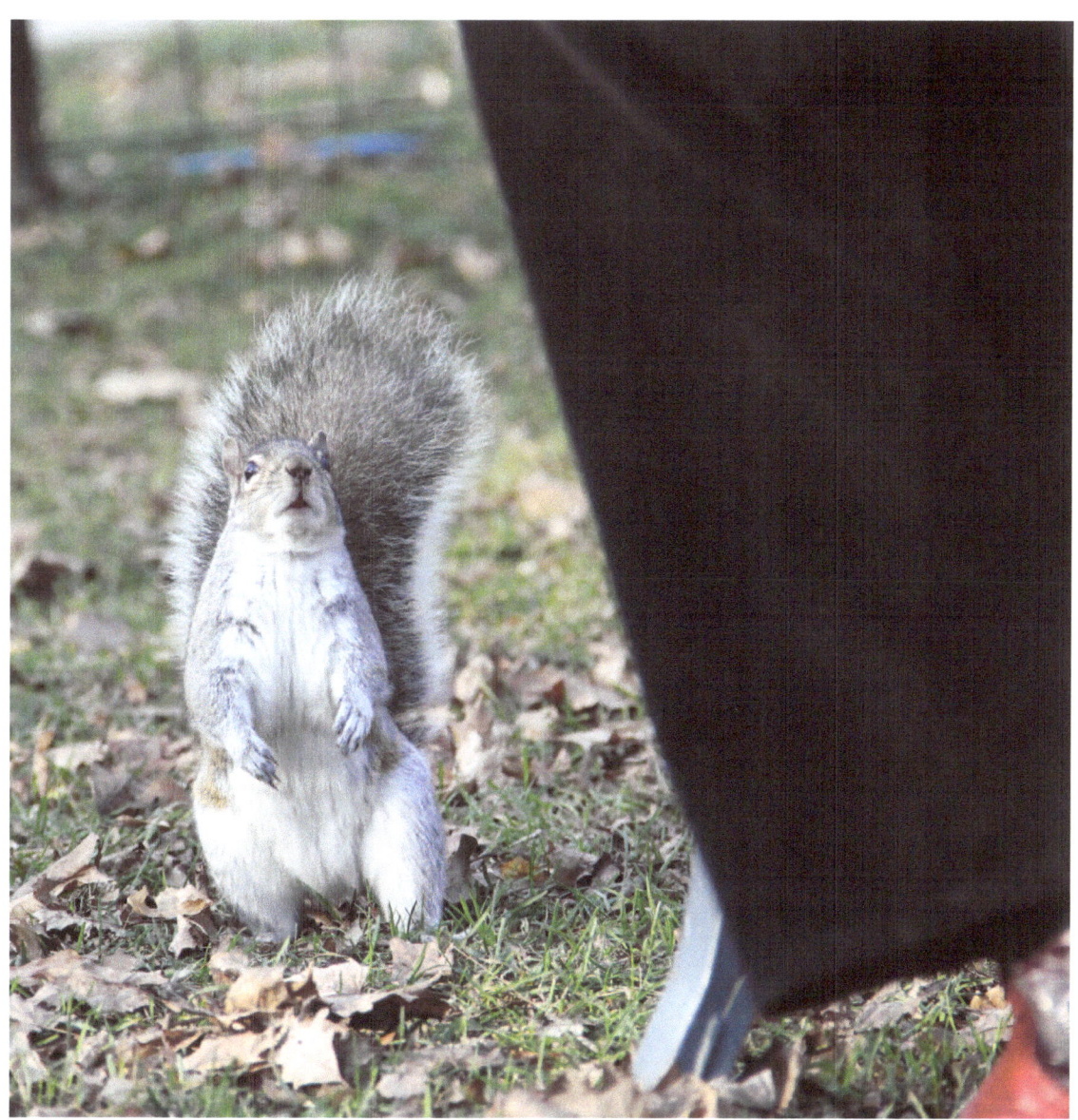

Sir, you've got some food for me too, please?

The Squirrels and I

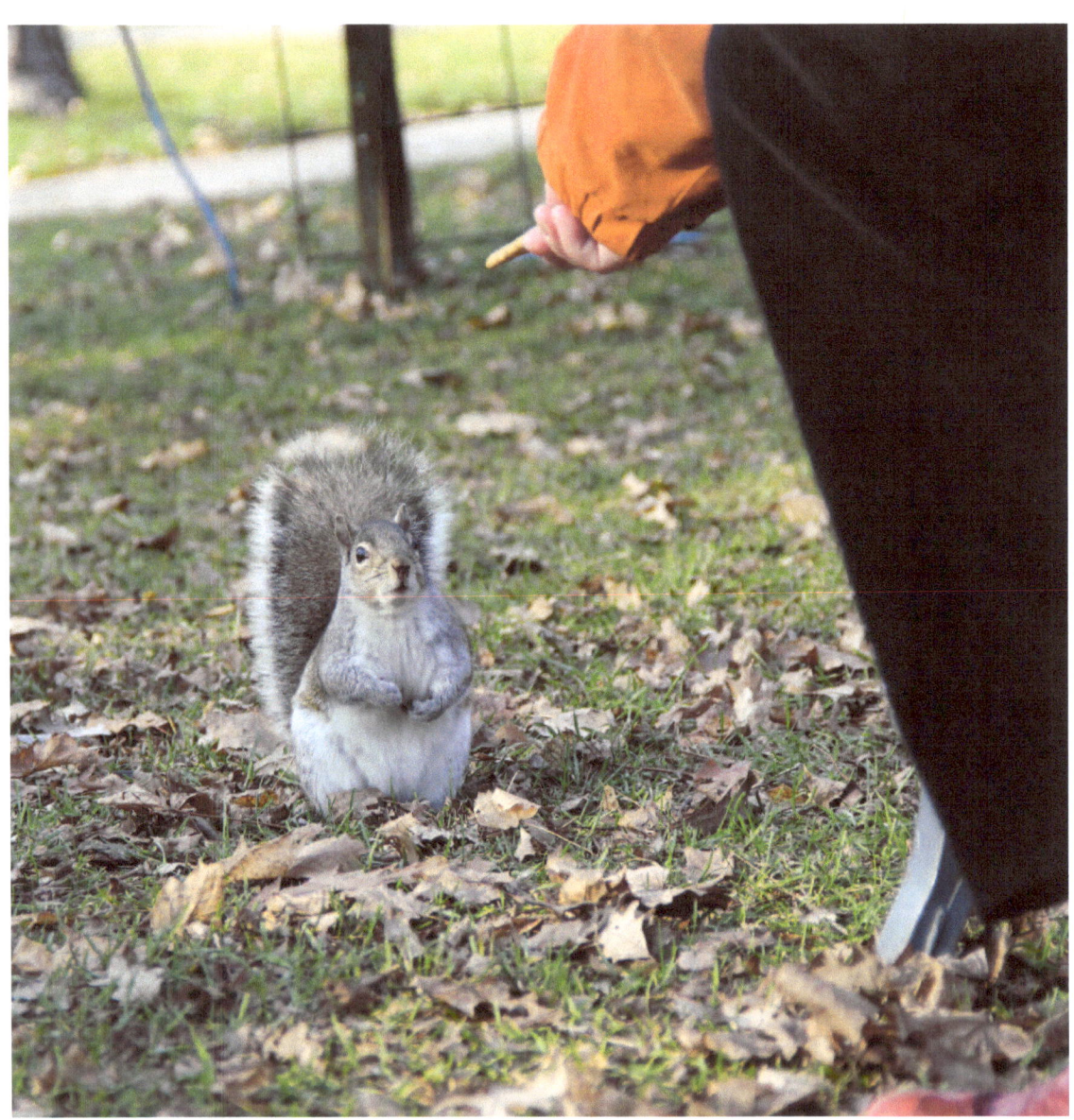

Of course ... Here, have a tea bicuit.

The Squirrels and I

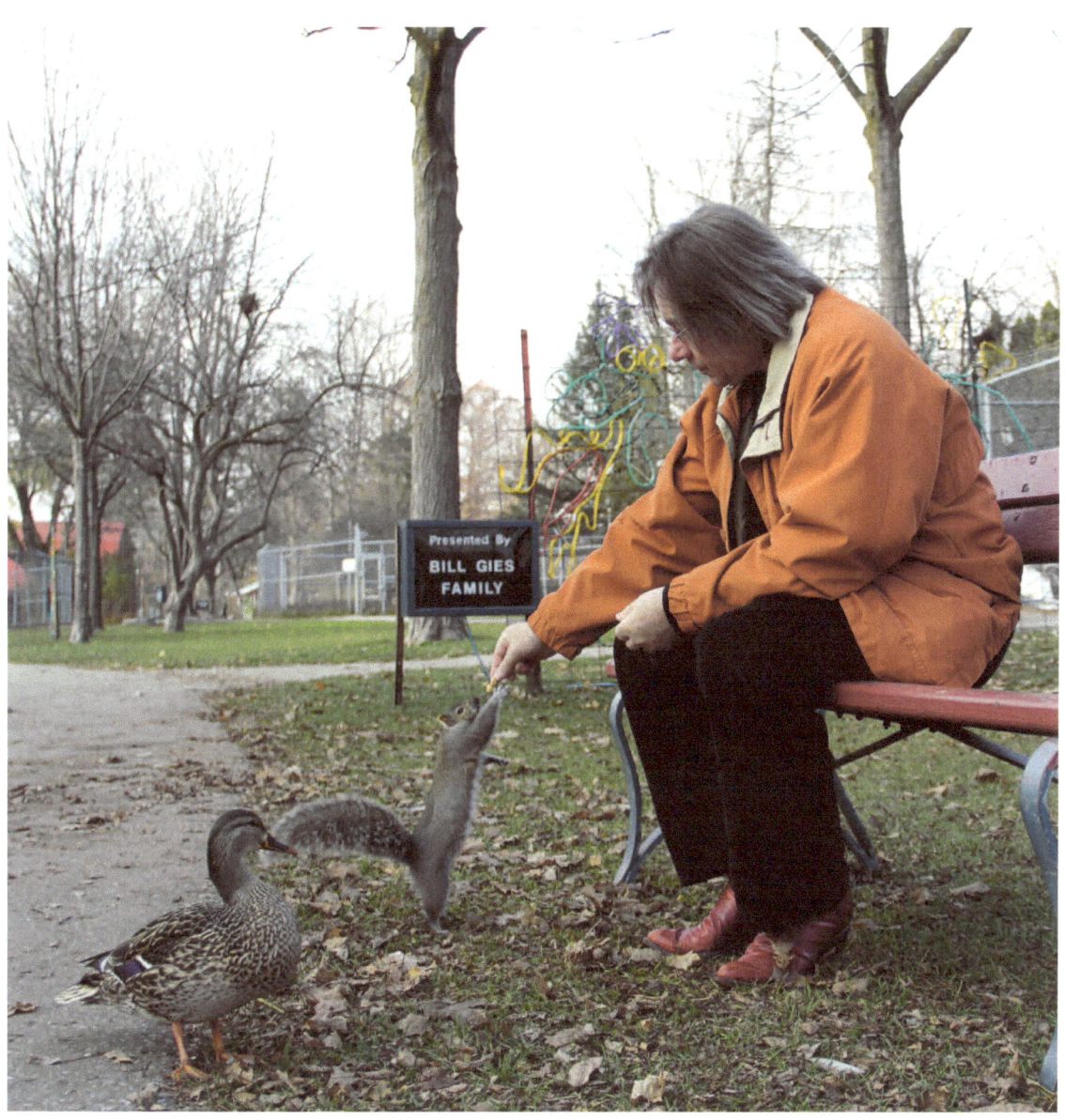

You want a peanut?

The Squirrels and I

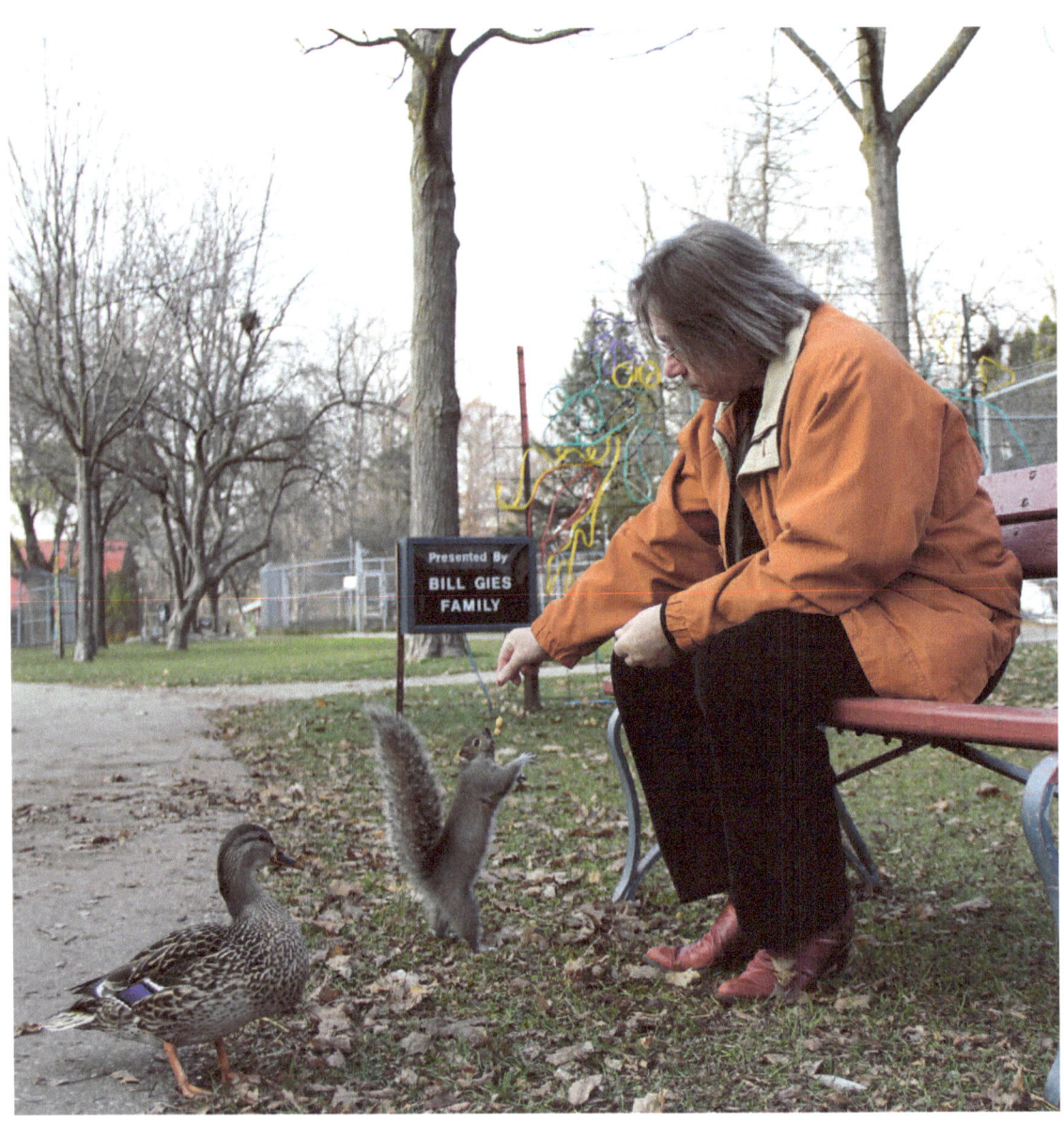

You have to catch it!

The Squirrels and I

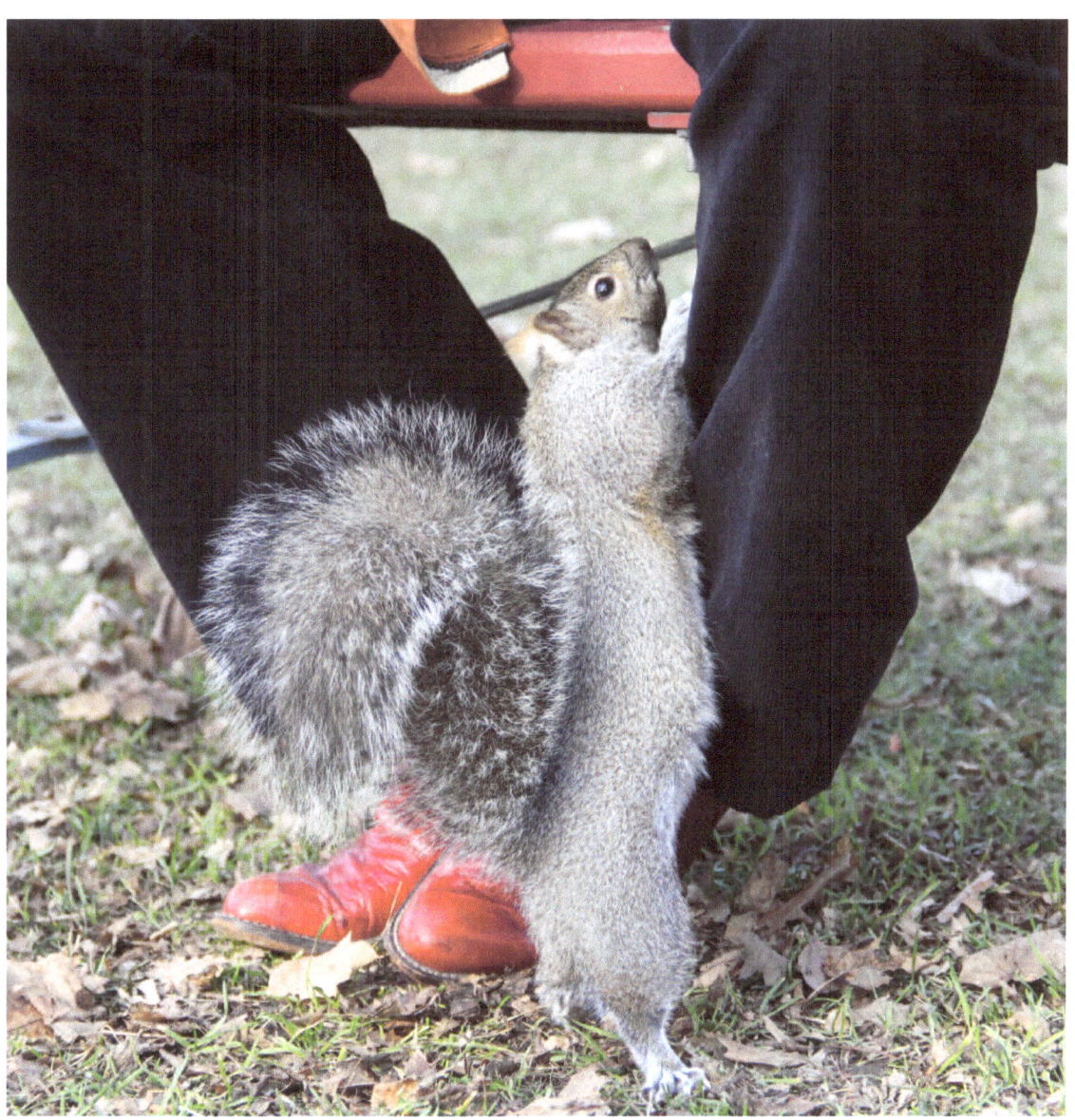

Thank you so much, Sir, for all the good food.

The Squirrels and I

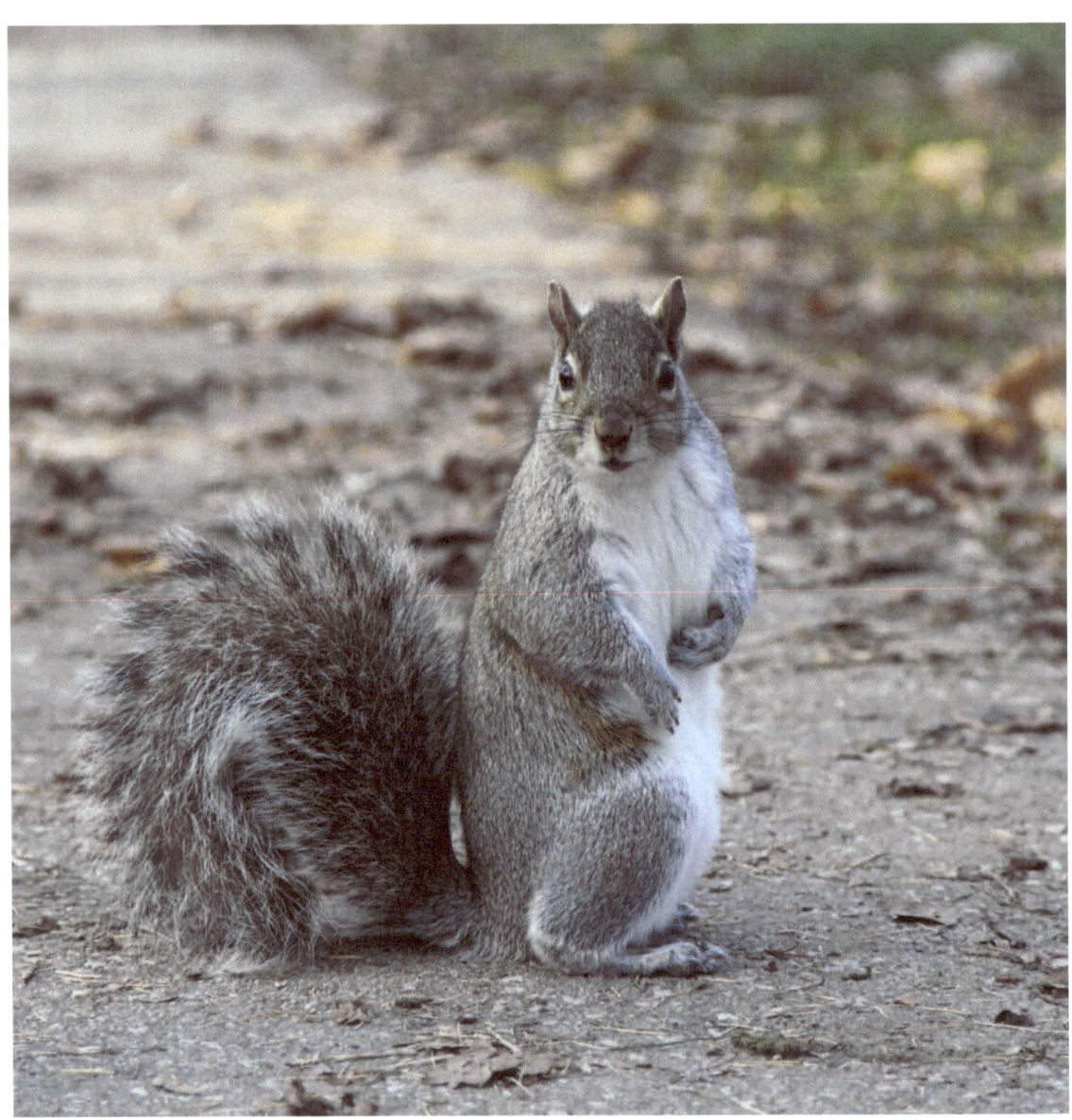

SORRY YOU HAVE TO LEAVE NOW.

The Squirrels and I

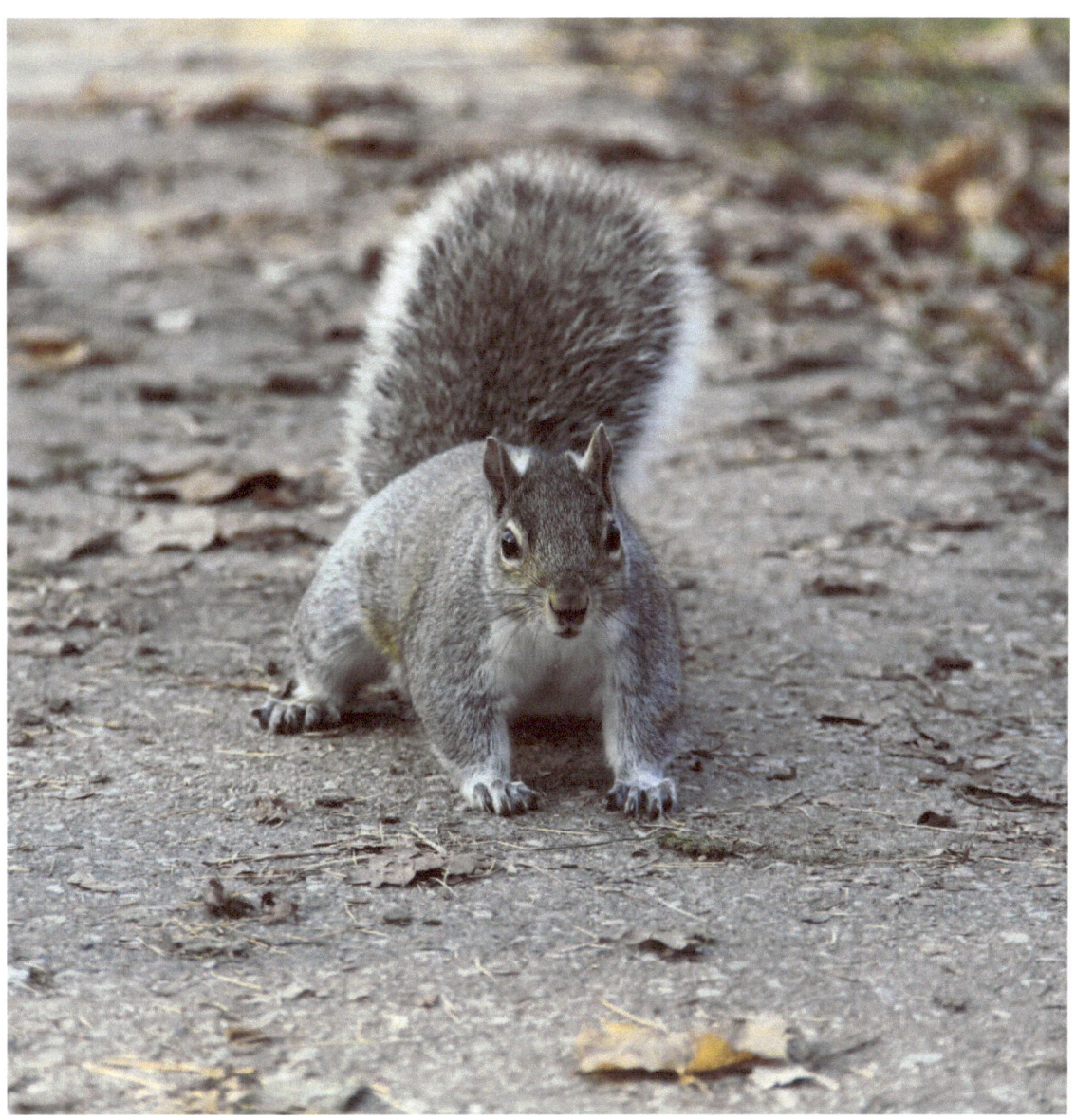

Please, come back soon. Winter is comming and we have to stock up our pantries.

BIBLIOGRAPHY—Klaus D. Emrich

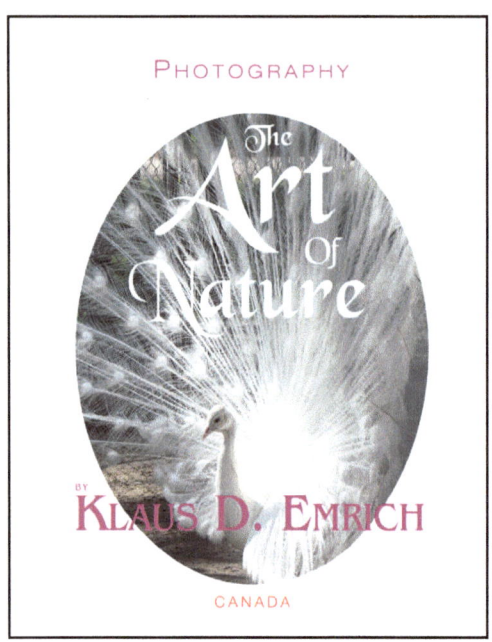

THE ART OF NATURE
Photography - Canadian nature.

BOOKS ALSO AVAILABLE IN GERMAN LANGUAGE.

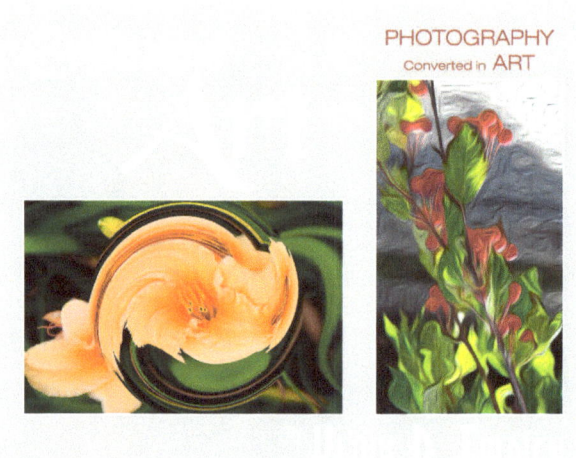

CREATIVE ART
Artistic view via photography.

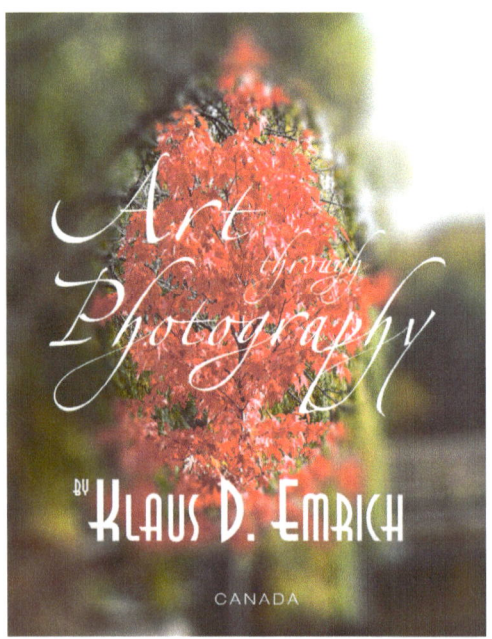

ART THROUGH PHOTOGRAPHY
Photography converted into art.

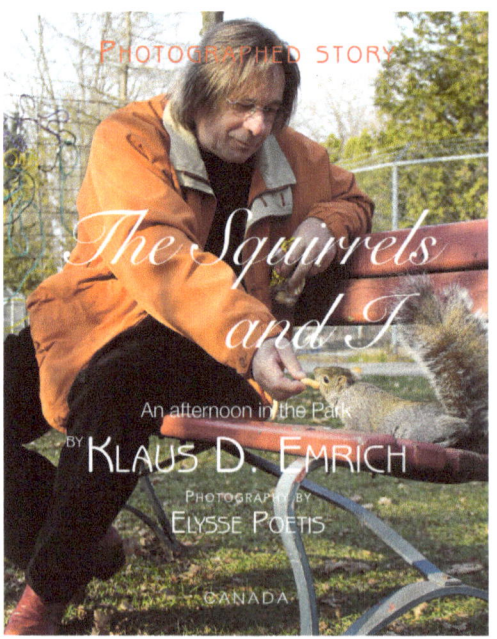

THE SQUIRRELS AND I
Photographed story.

ABOUT THE AUTHOR

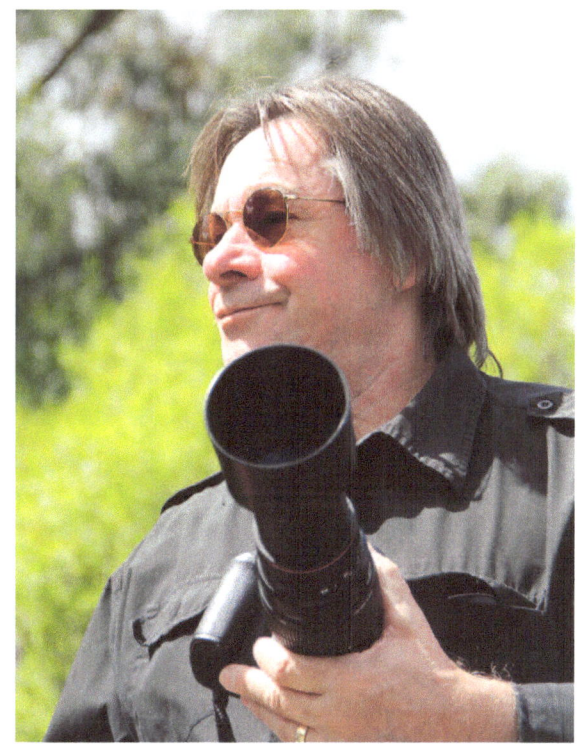

Klaus D. Emrich loved to create art since he was a small child back in Germany. He would explore nature's fields and just stare at its beauty. Only in recent years did Klaus started using his talent/imagination via art and photography. In many of his future books, just like in this one, Klaus is the model.

Creating beauty was always his greatest dream. This fun book, "The Squirrels and I," was published in September 2014 by Von Der Alps Publishing Corporation. Klaus D. Emrich is the author of multiple books on Amazon, with many more continuously being published.

Klaus and his wife Mary, (pseudonym Elysse Poetis - Award Winning author/poet/photographer of many books on Amazon), reside in the famous Region of Waterloo, Ontario, CANADA.

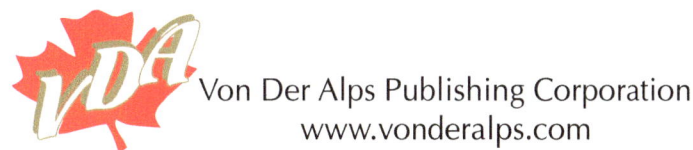 Von Der Alps Publishing Corporation
www.vonderalps.com